Frida Kahlo

She painted her world in self-portraits

Written by
Amy Guglielmo

Illustrated by
Natalia Rojas Castro

On July 6, 1907, a baby named Magdalena Carmen Frida Kahlo y Calderón was born in a blue house on Londres Street in Coyoacán, a region in Mexico City. She was the fifth of six daughters. Her family called her Frida.

Frida's father, Guillermo, was born in Germany, the son of a painter and goldsmith. When he was 19, he moved to Mexico, where he worked as a photographer. Frida's mother, Matilde, was born in Mexico of Spanish and Indigenous Mexican heritage.

At the blue house, *La Casa Azul*, the garden burst with blooming flowers, prickly pear cacti, and colorful tangles of vines. This was young Frida's favorite place to play and search for songbirds and hungry iguanas as they nibbled on the mango fruit.

When Frida was six years old, she fell ill with polio. In 1913, there were no vaccines to prevent the disease that caused her pain and made the muscles in her right leg weak. Frida's right leg became thinner and shorter than her left leg, and she had to stay in her room for nine months to recover.

During the day, Frida stared out from her bed and into the gardens, following the paths of butterflies as they fluttered from flower to flower.

At night, lonely Frida steamed up the windowpane of her room with her breath, traced a tiny door with her finger, and pretended to escape. Frida envisioned her body floating through the window, across the street where her imaginary friend lived. Together the girls danced and played.

When Frida returned to school, the other kids made fun of her limp and called her names. She wore extra pairs of socks and wrapped her frail leg in bandages, then hid it under long skirts.

But Frida's father encouraged her to become stronger. He taught her how to ride a bike, box, wrestle, swim, and climb trees.

Sometimes, Frida went to work with her father, and he taught her about the architecture of the historic buildings of Mexico that he photographed for his job. Guillermo showed Frida how to use a camera, how to find the proper light, and how to pose. Frida helped in the photo studio by delicately hand-coloring photos with a tiny brush. In photography, Frida found an early mode of artistic expression. She arranged special outfits when she sat for her father. In one family portrait, Frida slicked back her hair and dressed in a man's suit, complete with a pocket square and a tie.

Draw a picture or take a photo of an interesting building. What do you notice?

Frida and her father also shared a love of nature. Together, they went on walks in nearby parks to collect pebbles, leaves, and bugs, and then painted the scenes with watercolors. Frida brought her treasures home to examine them under a microscope, looked them up in books, and made scientific drawings.

Guillermo believed that, like boys, girls should have an education. At the time, most Mexican girls stayed at home to learn how to cook and clean. But not Frida.

In 1922, when Frida turned 15, she entered Mexico's top academy: The National Preparatory School.

Out of 2,000 students, Frida was one of just 35 girls. Frida loved reading, math, and history, but her favorite subject was science. She wanted to become a doctor to help other children like her.

> *"Earlier on I wanted to get into medicine, I was so interested in curing people, relieving them of their pain."*
>
> Frida Kahlo

At school, Frida became friends with a group of pranksters called the "*Cachuchas*" or the "Caps," after their matching caps. They loved books, music, poetry, and causing mischief. The group rode donkeys in the halls and lit off firecrackers to aggravate their teachers.

Across Mexico, after the Revolution (1910-1920), the government hired artists—like Diego Rivera—writers, and musicians to narrate the story of Mexico. Painters filled the walls of public buildings with large murals showing symbols, people, and places. The compositions celebrated episodes from the country's history.

Diego Rivera created one of these murals in the auditorium at Frida's school. Once, the Caps stole his lunch while he was working!

Frida tried her own prank on Diego and rubbed soap on the stairs below where he worked to make him slip, but he never did! Frida spent hours watching the artist at work.

Back home, Frida's family couldn't always afford to pay all their bills, and they had to sell some furniture to get by. To help her parents out, Frida took a job working as an assistant to a printmaker. There, Frida learned how to draw by copying the work of famous artists.

In her final year of high school—in September 1925—the bus Frida was riding got into a horrible accident. Frida was badly injured. Her spine was broken in three parts. She suffered collarbone and rib fractures, and broke three pelvic bones. Her right leg was fractured into multiple pieces, and her right foot was crushed.

> *"In this hospital, death dances around my bed at night."*
>
> Frida Kahlo

For a month, Frida had to stay in the hospital to recover. She had multiple surgeries and was wrapped in a plaster cast from her neck to her toes. Frida couldn't take her exams, and her dreams of becoming a doctor were dashed. She missed school and her friends and family. Once again, Frida was sick, alone, and stuck in bed.

In the hospital, Frida drew, wrote letters, and read books, but she grew frustrated and bored. When she ran out of paper, she drew birds, butterflies, and flowers on her cast. After several weeks, she was given a smaller cast and allowed to go home.

Back at *La Casa Azul*, Frida continued her recovery and stared out at the garden from her bed, longing to be a bird. She doodled on her new cast. When Frida's mother discovered her drawings, she had an idea.

Matilde gave Frida a paint box that once belonged to Guillermo and some paper. Frida drew her foot because it was all that she could see. Then, her mother had a special easel made, and Frida started painting everyone in her family. Eventually, she ran out of people and things to paint. Then, Frida's mother had another idea...

"Feet what do I need you for when I have wings to fly."

Frida Kahlo

Matilde had a mirror installed over Frida's bed. Frida was able to paint herself! She posed in the mirror, just like her father had taught her, capturing her thick eyebrows, her dark brown eyes, and her perfectly parted hair. Painting gave Frida the hope to be able to heal. She used her imagination to tell her story on each canvas, living—and growing stronger—through her art.

Be like Frida! Paint a picture of your foot. Capture the details in your toes.

As portrait after portrait lined the room, Frida was getting better, and so were her paintings. For two years, she stayed at home and painted more than 24 paintings. Soon, Frida knew exactly what she had to do. She had a new dream—to become an artist!

As soon as Frida was well enough, she started seeing friends again. She never returned to her old school, but she still hung out with the "Caps." She also made new friends who were interested in art, politics, and Mexican culture. She attended parties and participated in protests and marches.

Frida kept painting, but she needed to know if she was talented enough to earn money to pay her medical bills. By this time, Frida was 21 years old, and she wanted to hear the truth. So, in 1928, Frida took her three best paintings and boarded a bus into town in search of Mexico's most famous artist—the same artist that had painted the mural at her school.

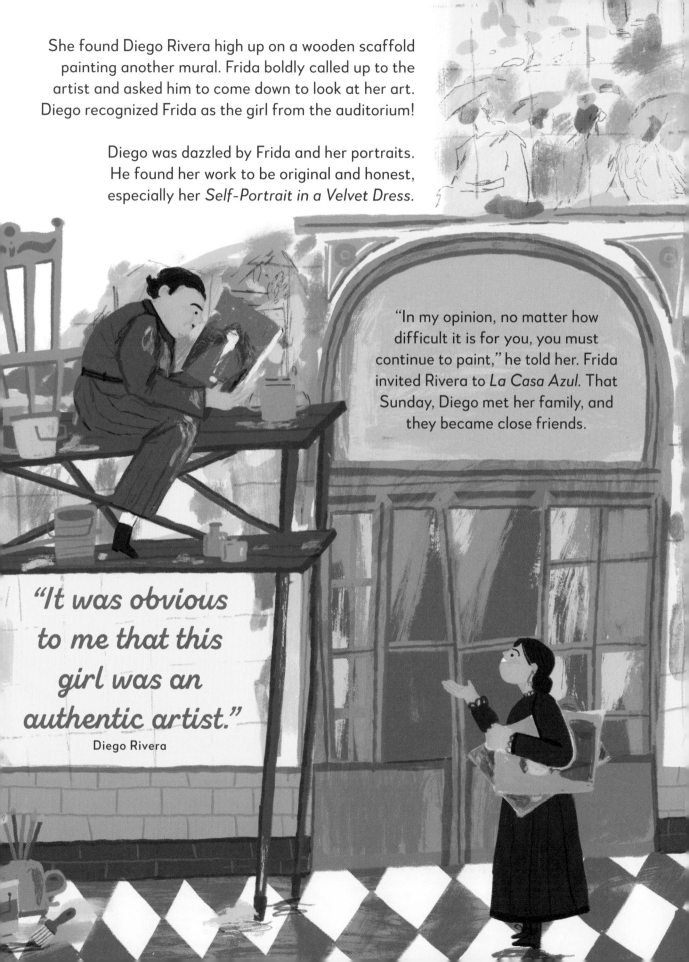

She found Diego Rivera high up on a wooden scaffold painting another mural. Frida boldly called up to the artist and asked him to come down to look at her art. Diego recognized Frida as the girl from the auditorium!

Diego was dazzled by Frida and her portraits. He found her work to be original and honest, especially her *Self-Portrait in a Velvet Dress*.

"In my opinion, no matter how difficult it is for you, you must continue to paint," he told her. Frida invited Rivera to *La Casa Azul*. That Sunday, Diego met her family, and they became close friends.

"It was obvious to me that this girl was an authentic artist."

Diego Rivera

By the late 1920s, Mexico City had become a place for artists, writers, musicians, and thinkers from around the world. They were attracted to the spirit of freedom that occurred after the Mexican Revolution. Frida was eager to join in the creative energy that was blossoming in the city. Diego and Frida's shared interest in friends, culture, and politics drew them closer together. They fell in love, and in 1929, when Frida was 22 years old, they were married!

The couple hosted many gatherings for their artist friends, and Frida prepared food for hours. In the early days of their marriage, Frida was so busy entertaining and cooking that she didn't have much time to paint.

In 1929, Diego and Frida moved south of Mexico City to Cuernavaca, where they both worked on their art. Enlivened by her new home, Frida wandered the countryside dotted with fragrant white oleander and banana trees. Frida was drawn to the Indigenous imagery and the bright, bold colors she saw being used by Diego.

Take a sketchbook outside and draw what you see!

Frida studied church paintings and sculptures, and Mexican folk art. She painted Indigenous women and children and more self-portraits. Frida added religious symbols, like angels, and objects, like clocks, into her vibrant compositions that combined fantasy with her childhood memories.

With her exposure to new surroundings, Frida adopted elements of Indigenous dress—with her own playful flair—to recognize her connection to Mexico, to her ancestors, and to nature.

What do you like to wear that makes you feel special?

Frida crafted her ornate new look so that it wove together her political beliefs, her disability, and her creativity. She decorated her body in layers of jangling, chunky jewelry, so people could hear when she entered a room. And to draw people's attention to her face, she colored her brows dark, braided her hair in brilliant ribbons, and wore elaborate headdresses (called *resplandors*), or magnificent flowers crowns. Traditional Mexican clothing—like square huipil blouses and patterned rebozo shawls—covered her back braces and medical corsets. Through her fashion choices, she both concealed and celebrated her ailments.

Frida spent hours arranging her look, picking the perfect jade necklaces, long, dangling earrings, and giant silver rings for every finger. Both in person and in her paintings, she carefully chose how to present herself. Frida was her own canvas, and she decorated herself with all the colors of the rainbow. Through her outfits she could be confident, funny, creative, and daring.

In late 1930, Diego was commissioned to make murals in several cities in the United States. Frida looked forward to the adventure. There were new people to meet and paint!

The artists set sail for San Francisco, where Diego would make two murals. Frida was amazed by this scenic city on the west coast of the US. She rode the trolleys, visited museums, and bought silk in the city's Chinatown. People marveled at her style. Renowned photographers and painters like Imogen Cunningham and Edward Weston asked her to pose for portraits. Frida was surrounded by writers and artists. Together, they would make art, talk politics, and sightsee.

The couple's next stop was New York City, where Diego was featured in a solo show at The Museum of Modern Art. In this city, Frida discovered a love for malted milkshakes, department stores, and the movie theater. On opening night at Diego's exhibition, Frida and her vivid garments stood out in a sea of patrons dressed all in black.

Try sketching a busy city scene. How many people can you draw?

When the couple traveled to Detroit, Frida experimented with printmaking and painting on metal, but it wasn't until she fell severely ill and spent many days in the hospital that her work became even more narrative. Her *Self-Portrait On the Borderline Between Mexico and the United States* showed her standing in two countries to portray her mixed emotions. Frida used the sun and moon to represent darkness and light and roots and flowers to show her connection to Mexico.

Diego was happy to be working, but Frida grew homesick and couldn't wait to get back to Mexico. After almost four years, the two artists sailed back home.

Back in Mexico City in 1934, the couple moved into a new home that they had designed. They each had their own house. Frida's was blue, and next door, Diego's house was pink. The two buildings were connected by a bridge.

At first, Frida was happy to be settling into her new space, but Diego grew restless and longed to go back to America. Diego blamed Frida for making him return to Mexico.

Once again, Frida's health worsened. She was admitted to the hospital for several operations and was not well enough to paint. As she recovered, Frida started a few drawings to lighten her mood. When they didn't turn out the way she liked, she tore them up!

Diego and Frida continued to argue, and they decided it was better to live apart. Frida was so upset that she cut off her long hair and stopped wearing the Mexican clothes that she had distinctively adopted. She painted her self-portraits to express her passionate feelings.

Frida painted herself with short hair to show her independence from the tradition for women to have long hair. She painted her family tree to celebrate her mixed heritage. She painted other women to share their journeys.

"I paint self-portraits because I am so often alone, because I am the person I know best."

Frida Kahlo

In her art, Frida focused on the personal. She used her heartbreak, humor, love, and memories to fuel her body of work. Through portraits, Frida kept telling her story. She kept painting, and painting, and painting...

Even though her foot and spine caused Frida agony, she refused to be pitied. She was eager to go out to see people and have fun. She loved to go to movies, concerts, and, most of all, to go dancing.

Throughout her life, Frida had a wide circle of friends who brought her joy and laughter. Her friends included the playwright Clare Boothe Luce and photographers Tina Modotti and Dorothea Lange. Like Frida, they were known for depicting powerful scenes of female experiences. Some of her friends were political figures like the Russian revolutionary Leon Trotsky, who arrived in Mexico in 1936.

In 1938, Frida was invited to exhibit some of her paintings in an art show at the University Gallery in Mexico City. Critics called her work interesting and innovative. A movie star who was an art collector bought four of her paintings.

When the French writer André Breton visited Mexico, he was fascinated by Frida's work. He convinced an art dealer friend in New York to give Frida her first solo exhibition. André was a member of an art group called the Surrealists who made images based on dreams and fantasy. He thought Frida's dreamlike paintings made her a Surrealist too, but Frida didn't like to be labeled.

> *"They thought I was a Surrealist, but I wasn't. I never painted dreams. I painted my own reality."*
>
> Frida Kahlo

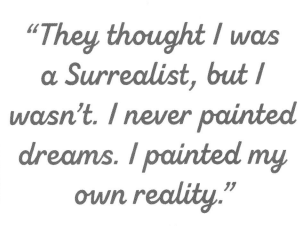

In 1938, Frida traveled to New York for the opening night of her show. Prominent artists were there, like Isamu Noguchi and Georgia O'Keeffe. Frida's distinctive style and artwork caused a splash in the art world, and her show was a wild success. She sold more than half of the 25 paintings on display.

In January of 1939, Frida sailed to Paris to participate in a gallery exhibition featuring Mexican art. At that time, Paris was an important center that attracted artists experimenting with ideas and forms of expression. Although the show was disappointing, Frida became friends with several other artists, including Pablo Picasso, Marcel Duchamp, Joan Miró, Wassily Kandinsky, the designer Elsa Schiaparelli, and performer Josephine Baker.

When Frida returned to Mexico, she and Diego weren't getting along, and they decided to get a divorce. Frida went back to *La Casa Azul*. On the day the divorce papers arrived, Frida completed one of her most notable paintings. *The Two Fridas* revealed the anguish of her loss with images of her broken heart. At this time, Frida had turned to painting nonstop and created some of her most famed pieces. Using symbols—like flags—to show her devotion to Mexico and animals—like doves—to represent peace, Frida made paintings that expressed hope and happiness but also gloom and sadness.

Diego and Frida promised to remain friends and saw each other often. At first, they continued to host parties, go to events, and paint together. But when Frida fell ill again, she retreated to bed and didn't work. Diego traveled to San Francisco to complete a mural. For three months, Frida was laid up in a plaster cast, unable to paint and full of despair. Both her body and heart were hurting.

In San Francisco, Diego missed Frida terribly and regretted their breakup. He included Frida in his mural *Pan-American Unity*. Diego arranged for Frida to fly to San Francisco for treatment.

Frida got better, and on December 8, 1940, in a small ceremony in San Francisco, she and Diego got married again!

What are your favorite animals? Make a colorful drawing of them in a natural setting.

In 1941, Frida and Diego moved into her childhood home, *La Casa Azul,* and added a new layer of blue paint, red window frames, and green doors. They filled the gardens with palms, ivy, ferns, guava trees, pink lilies, yellow sunflowers, golden marigolds, sweetly scented gardenias, and ancient Mexican sculptures. Frida made a cozy yellow kitchen that she decorated with objects she collected on her travels. She placed dolls, toys, skulls, piñatas, and various Mexican knickknacks throughout the home.

La Casa Azul was a lively space, and other artists, writers, and personalities visited often. A menagerie of pets wandered the courtyard and house. They included a fawn, a monkey, cats, turtles, ducks, geese, chirping parakeets, an eagle, several hairless dogs, and a parrot named Bonito. Frida called them her children.

As a couple, Frida and Diego were finally content in each other's company, working, sharing meals, and catching rays of sunshine on the patio. Frida's favorite animals, objects, and plants often appeared in her paintings. The magical house and garden were a source of comfort and joy and provided another form of artistic expression for Frida.

In the early 1940s, some of Frida's newest self-portraits were displayed in prestigious art exhibitions in Mexico City, Philadelphia, Boston, and New York. She was given several awards and honors. In 1943, in a signal of her international recognition, Frida was asked to teach art at La Esmerelda National School of Painting, Sculpture, and Engraving in Mexico City.

Draw a portrait of someone you see on the street.

Where do you think they are going?

Frida didn't feel like she was a qualified teacher, but her students were devoted. Frida took them on field trips to paint the colors, shapes, buildings, and people of the city. Frida became close with a group of four students who called themselves "*Los Fridos.*"

When the journey to the school became too much for her aching body, Frida invited the students to *La Casa Azul*. She would welcome them and say, "The whole garden is ours. Let's go paint!" The blue house awakened the imagination of her pupils.

"I am not sick. I am broken. But I am happy to be alive as long as I can paint."

Frida Kahlo

By the end of 1944, Frida needed to have additional surgeries on her spine and foot. Frida was given a steel corset to support her back, the first of 28 corsets she wore during this period. Some were plaster, some were leather, and some she painted. All were very painful. The treatments caused her much mental anguish as well. Frida worked from her bed and painted herself wounded and in corsets. By translating her pain onto canvas, she found relief.

In 1950, Frida spent a year in the hospital, and Diego stayed in a room next door. Friends visited the hospital and, together, they watched funny movies and ate feasts. When Frida was able to return home, she was in a wheelchair. She painted from her bed, working on still life paintings of native fruit and arranged objects. She said it was easier for her to paint things that didn't move! In her compositions, watermelons mirrored the colors of the Mexican flag, and fruit and plants symbolized both life and death.

"At the end of the day, we can endure much more than we think we can."

Frida Kahlo

Frida's bed had become her world, and she decorated it with photographs, trinkets, flowers, and even a full-size skeleton on the top of her canopy. The skeleton was her reminder to keep living!

In 1953, Frida was given news that her work would be featured in a monographic show, meaning that it would feature her works and no other artist's! It was the first exhibition in Mexico that was devoted to her works. Frida sent out invitations to everyone she knew.

Frida's exhibition opened at The Gallery of Contemporary Art in Mexico City. Frida's doctors warned her that she was too sick to attend, but Frida didn't listen. She arranged for her four-poster bed to be moved to the gallery and entered the show on a stretcher. Fully made up with red lips and nails, Frida wore a crown of flowers and ribbons, jewels, and colorful scarves. In her thronelike bed, Frida became part of the show. Once again, she had caused a sensation! The gallery was a fiesta filled with laughter, music, singing, and friends.

"There is nothing more precious than laughter—it is strength to laugh and lose oneself, to be light."

Frida Kahlo

The exhibition was a triumph and was extended for a month. Frida was amazed and thrilled, but she was also tired and fading. That same year, doctors had to amputate the bottom of her right leg. She had a prosthetic leg custom-made out of a bright red boot, complete with a dragon design and bells.

A few months later, just after her 47th birthday in 1954, Frida died in her sleep at *La Casa Azul*.

Frida's coffin was brought to the Palace of Fine Arts and covered in red flowers. Hundreds of mourners came to pay their respects, and more than 500 people escorted her coffin to the grave. Frida's final painting was a still life of watermelons with the words *"Viva la vida,"* which translates to "Long live life!"

In the 1970s–1990s, Frida's paintings were rediscovered by art historians. Both the artist and her art started to become iconic symbols of feminism and women's contribution to the arts. Exhibitions, movies, plays, and books—including her diary—celebrated the life of this daring, original artist. *La Casa Azul* is now a museum with approximately 25,000 visitors every month.

Frida y Diego
vivieron en
esta casa
1929–1954

Frida's life was filled with challenges, but she found the strength to transform her pain and create art. Frida shared her vibrant, passionate life on her canvases. Her works continue to delight and inspire viewers around the world.

"Painting completed my life."

Frida Kahlo

Timeline of key artworks

During her career, Frida famously created numerous portraits and still life paintings. In all her works, she painted in her unique style using objects, symbols, and colors to represent important memories in her life. Here are a few key pieces from Frida's lifetime of work.

1926
*Self-Portrait in
a Velvet Dress*

1931
Frida and
Diego Rivera

> *"There is nothing absolute. Everything changes, everything moves, everything revolves, everything flies and goes away."*
>
> Frida Kahlo

1932
Self-Portrait On the
Borderline Between
Mexico and the
United States

1941
Self-Portrait with Bonito

1946
The Wounded Deer

1954
Viva la Vida

Make a self-portrait!

Of the 200 paintings Frida Kahlo made in her lifetime, more than 50 were self-portraits! Frida used her self-portraits to tell her story. She carefully chose her jewelry, costumes, and hairstyles for each painting to share her emotions. Sometimes she added her favorite animals, like her pet monkey, Fulang Chang, and Bonito, her pet parrot.

Frida's early self-portraits, like *Self-Portrait in a Velvet Dress*, were painted in the style of famous painters that came before her. Frida eventually developed her own style when she started painting herself with bold, bright colors and symbols, scenery, and objects that were meaningful to her life. Many of Frida's portraits were joyful and bright, but Frida also painted herself as a wounded deer in a forest to portray her emotional and physical pain.

1938
The Frame

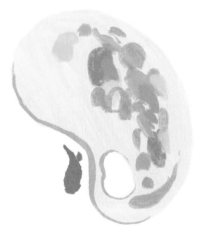

"In spite of my illness, I feel immense joy in LIVING."

Frida Kahlo

Be like Frida! Become a work of art! Before you start, dress yourself in your favorite outfit to make your self-portrait unique. What will you be wearing?

Now it's your turn!

First, find a mirror and study your reflection.

Next, use a pencil to sketch an oval for your face, then add lines for your neck and the outline of your clothing. Draw the details of your eyes, nose, mouth, eyebrows, and hair or a special hat!

Add a few drawings of objects—like your pet, sports equipment, or other favorite things or places—in the background. What are the objects that you will include in your self-portrait?

Fill in your sketch using crayons, paint, colored pencils, or markers to make it come to life!

Try this yourself!

Bold and Bright Still Life

Throughout her career, Frida painted still life paintings of arranged objects, including fruit and flowers. Frida painted many when she was sick in bed, because it was easier for her to paint things that didn't move. Frida's final painting was a still life of watermelons with the words "*Viva la vida*," which means "Long live life!"

Like her self-portraits, some of Frida's still life paintings included her pets and other animals, like owls and doves. Sometimes, she also included symbols, plants, words, flags, and scenery in her work. Some of Frida's favorite foods to paint included melons, tomatoes, coconuts, mangos, and oranges.

1954
Viva la Vida

Frida painted several still life paintings as gifts. Who would you give a still life painting to?

Your turn!

Challenge yourself!

Find some objects that would make a nice arrangement. You can use fruit and flowers, like Frida, or you can find your favorite food, books, toys, or other things that help tell your story.

What are some colorful items that you can add to your still life?

Place the items in a way that you can draw them together. Use pens, pencils, or crayons to sketch your still life. Next, use paint, colored pencils, or markers to make your sketches bright and bold.

Frida made some of her still life paintings round. Cut a piece of paper in the shape of a circle to try it! Test different background colors and papers to get different results. Make different groupings and objects to make a whole series of still life paintings.

You can add a colorful paper frame to make your still life really shine!

Glossary

Composition
The arrangement of elements in a painting or other work of art.

Indigenous
The people who are the original or
earliest known inhabitants of an area.

Mural
A painting or other work of art created directly on a wall.

Polio
Poliomyelitis is a disease caused by a virus.
There is now a vaccine to prevent polio.

Printmaking
The process of transferring images onto
a flat surface like cloth or paper.

Self-portrait
A representation of themself
created by an artist.

Still Life
A painting or drawing of an arrangement
of objects, often flowers, fruits, or vases.

Surrealism
An international movement that started in the 1920s,
and included writers and artists who prioritized the
unconscious and dreams over the familiar and everyday.

Symbolism
The use of an object or a word to
represent an abstract idea.

Mexican Revolution (1910–1920)
The Revolution started in 1910, when poor and
working-class people fought against the government
and wealthy landowners for fair pay, equal rights,
and better opportunities for their families. The
battle was successful, and the Constitution of
Mexico was written in 1917.

Amy Guglielmo

Amy Guglielmo is an author, educator, artist, and community arts and STEAM advocate. She has written many books for children, including *Cezanne's Parrot* and *Just Being Dali: The Story of Artist Salvador Dali*. Amy has coauthored the picture books *Pocket Full of Colors: The Magical World of Mary Blair*, winner of the Christopher Award; *How to Build a Hug: Temple Grandin and Her Amazing Squeeze Machine*; and the *Touch the Art* series of novelty board books featuring famous works of art with tactile additions. She lives in New York and Mexico with her husband.

Natalia Rojas Castro

Natalia Rojas Castro is an illustrator based in Bogota, Colombia. She studied visual arts and animation and now works as an illustrator, although she likes to experiment with different media for her images. Like Frida, the inspiration for her work is life itself, self-portraits that speak of her feelings, and Latin landscapes full of nature and color. When she is not working in her studio, she likes to go hiking in the mountains and draw what surrounds her.

Penguin Random House

Project Editor Rosie Peet
Editor Vicky Armstrong
US Senior Editor Jennette ElNaggar
Project Art Editor Chris Gould
Art Director Clare Baggaley
Production Editor Siu Yin Chan
Production Controller Louise Minihane
Senior Acquisitions Editor Katy Flint
Managing Art Editor Vicky Short
Publishing Director Mark Searle

First American Edition, 2023
Published in the United States by DK Publishing
1745 Broadway, 20th Floor, New York, NY 10019

Page design copyright © 2023 Dorling Kindersley Limited
DK, a Division of Penguin Random House LLC
23 24 25 26 27 10 9 8 7 6 5 4 3 2 1
001–333560–Dec/2023

 **The Metropolitan
Museum of Art**
New York

©The Metropolitan Museum of Art

All rights reserved.
Without limiting the rights under the copyright reserved above, no part of this
publication may be reproduced, stored in or introduced into a retrieval system,
or transmitted, in any form, or by any means (electronic, mechanical,
photocopying, recording, or otherwise), without the prior written
permission of the copyright owner.
Published in Great Britain by Dorling Kindersley Limited

A catalog record for this book
is available from the Library of Congress.
ISBN 978-0-7440-7069-9

DK books are available at special discounts when purchased
in bulk for sales promotions, premiums, fund-raising, or educational use.
For details, contact: DK Publishing Special Markets,
1745 Broadway, 20th Floor, New York, NY 10019
SpecialSales@dk.com

Printed and bound in Latvia

Acknowledgments
DK would like to thank Stephen Mannello and Brinda Kumar at The Met;
Martin Copeland and Myriam Meguarbi for picture research;
and Sarah Harland for proofreading.
The author would like to thank Rita and Alex.

www.dk.com
www.metmuseum.org

MIX
Paper | Supporting
responsible forestry
FSC™ C018179
www.fsc.org

This book was made with Forest
Stewardship Council™ certified
paper—one small step in DK's
commitment to a sustainable future.
**For more information go to
www.dk.com/our-green-pledge**

Picture credits
The publisher would like to thank the following for additional permission to reproduce the copyrighted works of art:
(Key: a-above; b-below/bottom; c-center; f-far; l-left; r-right; t-top)

40 Bridgeman Images: © Photo: Jorge Contreras Chace / © Banco de México Diego Rivera Frida Kahlo Museums Trust, Mexico, D.F. / DACS 2023.
41 akg-images: © Banco de México Diego Rivera Frida Kahlo Museums Trust, Mexico, D.F. / DACS 2023 (b). Bridgeman Images: © Banco de México Diego Rivera Frida Kahlo Museums Trust, Mexico, D.F. / DACS 2023 (tl). **42** Bridgeman Images: Photo © Fine Art Images / © Banco de México Diego Rivera Frida Kahlo Museums Trust, Mexico, D.F. / DACS 2023. **43** Bridgeman Images: © Banco de México Diego Rivera Frida Kahlo Museums Trust, Mexico, D.F. / DACS 2023 (b); Photo © Fine Art Images / © Banco de México Diego Rivera Frida Kahlo Museums Trust, Mexico, D.F. / DACS 2023 (t). **44** Bridgeman Images: Photo © Fine Art Images / © Banco de México Diego Rivera Frida Kahlo Museums Trust, Mexico, D.F. / DACS 2023 (r). **46** Bridgeman Images: © Banco de México Diego Rivera Frida Kahlo Museums Trust, Mexico, D.F. / DACS 2023 (cl).